If You Lived Here

HOUSES of the WORLD

GILES LAROCHE

Clarion Books
An Imprint of HarperCollins*Publishers*
Boston   New York

If you lived here, in this dogtrot log house, you would have to step outside to get from your bedroom to the kitchen. Your family's sleeping area would be in one section of the house while the kitchen and living area would be in the other. Between the two sections would be an open hall with a floor where a dog could sleep or an opossum could scurry through. If you lived here, so could you.

HOUSE TYPE: Dogtrot or possumtrot log house. Early American pioneers built log houses quickly and easily from the trees they felled to create farmland. Since it was difficult to find straight logs longer than 16 feet that were not too heavy for the pioneers to lift, two separate spaces roughly 16 feet square under one roof made the house larger.

MATERIALS: The walls and chimneys of dogtrot log houses were made of logs notched together at the corners with the same handmade ax used to cut down the trees from the surrounding forest. Stones, sticks, mud, and even moss filled any gaps between the logs to keep out cold air. Log houses usually had bare earth floors. Over time, wood planks covered the dirt floors, and stone or brick chimneys replaced the

original log chimneys, which might catch fire.

LOCATION: Dogtrot log houses were built in the forests and mountains of the mid-Atlantic and southern colonies of America.

DATE: Dogtrots were very popular as the country expanded south and west in the 1700s and 1800s. Today's log homes are larger and much more comfortable than the old dogtrots and are usually built in rural, forested, and wilderness areas.

FASCINATING FACT: Seven United States presidents lived in log houses: James Polk, Zachary Taylor, Millard Fillmore, James Buchanan, Abraham Lincoln, Ulysses S. Grant, and James Garfield.

If you lived here, on this snowy mountain, you could shelter sheep, goats, and cows in your family's chalet. With as many as four floors, a chalet is much larger than the American dog-trot log house. Your animals would live on the ground level while you and your brothers and sisters sleep high above on the very top floor. Your skis, snowshoes, and ice skates would be placed under the lowest balcony by the entry door, and your homemade cheese stored in the cellar.

HOUSE TYPE: Chalet, from the French word *châtelet,* which means "small castle." The low-pitched roofs of chalets are covered with snow during the winter months, which traps the fireplace heat inside. The wide eaves above the balconies keep melting snow off the walls and balconies.

MATERIALS: The chalet's framework, floors, and siding were made from logs cut in nearby forests. A flat stone called slate, quarried from local mountains, made long-lasting roof tiles. Carvings and painted designs decorated the eaves and balconies.

LOCATION: Mountainous regions of Switzerland, Austria, Germany, France, and Scandinavia

DATE: Chalets were first built by Swiss farmers in the 1100s. Their design has a modern look that is often copied today, especially in ski resorts worldwide. This chalet was built in the 1840s.

FASCINATING FACT: Logs from trees felled in winter were thought to last longer than those cut in other seasons.

If you lived here, you'd need to scramble up a ladder to get to the hidden rooftop opening to enter your house. Instead of logs, your house would be built of adobe clay, and it would share walls with other homes to create a structure up to five stories high that from a distance would look like a village. If unwelcome visitors appeared, you could pull the ladder up behind you.

HOUSE TYPE: Pueblo, Spanish for "small village." The original builders, the Tiwa people, called their villages *teotho*.

MATERIALS: Thick adobe walls kept the pueblos cool in summer and warm in winter. The roof was made of pine logs with earth placed on top, and the movable ladders prevented invading nomadic tribes from getting inside easily.

LOCATION: The Sangre de Christo Mountains of Taos, New Mexico, and other sites in the arid southwestern states where there were few trees.

DATE: 1200s to the present. Adobe houses are still popular among Native Americans, as well as others who admire the building style. Though doors have been added and there are no longer invaders, some people still prefer to use ladders.

FASCINATING FACT: In the 1500s the Spanish taught the native Tiwa people how to form the adobe clay into sun-dried bricks, which were more durable and easier to build with than unformed clay.

If you lived here, you could get up from your bed in the main house, have breakfast in the back house kitchen, and then walk to the barn without ever having to go outside. The connecting rooms make it possible for you to take care of your animals without having to trudge through the deep snow and howling winds of winter. Doors would prevent the cows, goats, chickens, and geese from coming to visit you!

HOUSE TYPE: Connected barn. The original builders did not have a name for what we today call connected or continuous barns. However, part of a child's verse of the day, "big house, little house, back house, barn," describes them perfectly.

MATERIALS: Wood from local sawmills was used for the framing, house clapboards, barn boards, and roof shingles. Granite blocks or boulders formed the foundation, and the chimneys were made of brick.

LOCATION: Common in the northeastern United States

DATE: Construction of connected barns reached a peak in the decades after the Civil War, when farming flourished. Although no longer built, many connected barns survive as working farms.

FASCINATING FACT: Connected barns were often positioned so the back faced the cold north winds and the front opened onto a protected barnyard facing the sunny south side.

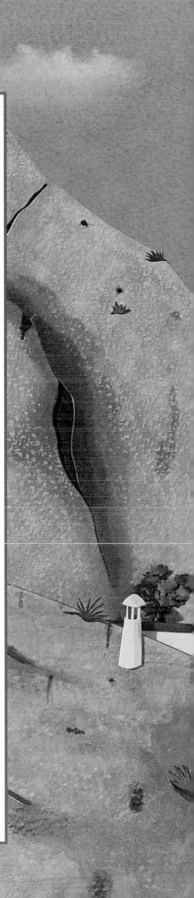

If you lived here, your bedroom would be inside a mountain. The front of your house, with its windows and doors, would hide the fact that your home is actually a cave dwelling. A chimney from the kitchen would poke up from the hillside above, and if another room was needed, your family could just carve one out of the interior's soft rock. Then you would be among the 45 million troglodytes (cave dwellers) living in the world today.

HOUSE TYPE: Cave dwelling

MATERIALS: The soft rock, called tufa, is easily carved and dries quickly when exposed to air. Bricks covered with stucco and terra cotta tiles are used for the façades (fronts) of the house. Like adobe clay, the tufa walls maintain a comfortable temperature year round. With no roof and few walls to construct, cave dwellings are inexpensive to build, and they blend into the landscape.

LOCATION: Barrio de los Cuevas ("village of the caves"), Guadix, and throughout Granada province in Andalucia, Spain. Other cave dwellings can be found in the southwestern United States, Turkey, China, and Pakistan.

DATE: Humans have lived in caves since prehistoric times. First built in the 1500s, the cuevas in the shadows of Spain's Sierra Nevada mountains are today home to more than 12,000 people. Today's cave dwellings often have multistoried modern interiors.

FASCINATING FACT: Many children growing up in villages with cave dwellings believe everyone lives in caves — and are surprised to discover that most people live in houses with a roof and four walls!

If you lived here, you could catch fish from your bedroom window. Tall and strong wooden stilts would hold your house high above the rising tides of an inlet of the Pacific Ocean. At high tide you could hop on a boat to visit a friend, and at low tide you could walk around the base of the stilts to gather crabs, or watch pelicans glide overhead in their own search for fish.

HOUSE TYPE: Palafitos (house on stilts) are built by fishermen above tidal waters to provide quick access to their boats moored below.

MATERIALS: Constructed almost entirely of wood from pine, larch, and cinnamon trees. The wood from Luma trees, which some-times grow in water, is very durable and often used for the stilts.

LOCATION: Chiloé Island, Chile. There are also houses on stilts in Asia, Europe, Africa, and elsewhere in South America.

DATE: 1500s to the present. The palafitos shown here were built in the 1900s.

FASCINATING FACT: Palafitos are quickly built as a community project by neighborhood families on special work days called *mingas*.

If you lived here, you would step directly from your front door onto a boat to go to school. Your neighborhood would be on a man-made island, barely above sea level, with a network of canals filled with all types of boat traffic instead of cars, bicycles, and buses. The floors of the three upper stories of your house are made of wood and tile, but the floor of the bottom story is water!

HOUSE TYPE: Venetian palace

MATERIALS: Huge wooden logs (pilings) driven into the mud support the wood and brick framework above. Stucco, plaster, and other, finer materials such as marble were used for the exterior and interior.

LOCATION: Grand Canal, Venice, Italy. The unique "floating city" of Venice was built in the shallow tidal lagoons of the Adriatic Sea, initially for protection from Barbarians who invaded over land and had no boats. It later became one of the wealthiest and most powerful cities in the world.

DATE: The Palazzo Darlo, shown here, was built in the 1200s and was remodeled in the 1490s. Later it became a hotel but is once again a private home.

FASCINATING FACT: The boat that takes you to school is called a gondola and is rowed by a standing oarsman called a gondolier. In 2010, a twenty-four-year-old became the first woman to qualify to be a gondolier in the 900-year history of the gondola.

If you lived here, you'd have to cross three drawbridges to get into your house, called a chateau. Once inside, you would have endless corridors with dozens of rooms to run through and seven towers to climb, from which you could see for miles. In the surrounding pond, called a moat, you could row alongside paddling ducks and swans, and over swimming frogs and turtles.

HOUSE TYPE: A chateau looks like a castle but is more comfortable and less fortress-like. But when the drawbridge is raised, it is almost impossible for anyone to get inside.

MATERIALS: Local granite was quarried for the supporting structure and marble, wood, and tile was used for the interior.

LOCATION: This chateau, called La Brède, is near Bordeaux, in southwest France.

DATE: Thousands of French chateaux were built from medieval times to the modern era. Construction of La Brède began in 1419, and additions were made in the 1500s. The chateau is shown here in the 1700s when it was owned by the famous writer Montesquieu. It was lived in by his descendants until 2004, when it became a museum.

FASCINATING FACT: The tall cone-shaped roofs of a chateau's towers are thought by the French to resemble witches' hats.

If you lived here, you would always have friends at home to play with because your huge round house would be home to dozens of families. Your family's own living and sleeping rooms would be on the upper levels, while cooking and laundry would be shared with others on the ground level. The interior rooms face inward onto courtyards, and only the two top floors have exterior windows.

HOUSE TYPE: Fujian tulou (earthen dwelling or "rammed-earth" dwelling). Tulous could also be square, oblong, octagonal, and large like a whole town or small like a village. In China it is often the custom for extended or even unrelated families to live together. Sharing living space and household duties reduces costs, and living in one building provides security in times of trouble.

MATERIALS: Primary building materials include a mixture of compacted fine sand, lime, and soil for the exterior walls. Stone blocks, bricks, and wood were used for the internal structure.

LOCATION: Hangkeng village, Yongding China. This example is called Zhen Cheng Lou (Inspiring Success Tower)

DATE: Tulous have been built for over 500 years. Zhen Cheng Lou, built in 1912, is today a UNESCO World Heritage Site.

FASCINATING FACT: Tulous are designed to withstand natural forces. For earthquake protection, the thick base walls become thinner and lighter in height, and the round shape allows strong winds to flow easily around the walls.

If you lived here, you could run downstairs to the ground floor to get pretzels and fresh-baked bread from your mom and dad's bakery. Your home would be separated from neighboring houses with walls that extend from the foundation to the very steep roof. From your bedroom under this roof, you could awaken to the sounds of cuckoos in nearby forests and the bustle of street activity below.

HOUSE TYPE: Half-timbered townhouses. Most of these houses had the family's business on the street level. Because these villages were so compact, getting across town — even by foot — was quick and easy.

MATERIALS: This building style developed where wood was plentiful and because wooden houses were cheaper to construct than those made of stone. When you look at the houses from the street, their structure is visible, much like an x-ray that shows a skeleton.

LOCATION: Miltenberg am Main, Germany, and other countries in northern Europe

DATE: These houses date from the 1530s, but half-timber construction was popular from the 1100s to the 1900s. People still live and shop in half-timbered houses.

FASCINATING FACT: Owners had to pay taxes based on the square footage of the ground floor. When the upper stories project over the walls below, these floors have more space without causing higher taxes.

If you lived here, how would you find your home when so many look alike? The color of the door and railing, flowerpots on the stairs, or your father standing on the balcony would help you spot your house. These cube-shaped houses seem to sit on top of each other as they mount up a steep hill. Because streets are often used like outdoor rooms, you might have to dart across a tiny lane to go from your bedroom to the kitchen!

HOUSE TYPE: Often called "white towns," the whitewashed village houses are clustered together for protection from the strong seasonal winds of the Aegean Sea.

MATERIALS: The walls are made of local stone and bricks covered with plaster. In summer the walls, stairs, roofs — even the stones of the streets — are brilliantly whitewashed to reflect the intense heat of the sun.

LOCATION: Astipalaia Island, Greece. Similar villages are found on other Greek islands and elsewhere in the Mediterranean Sea.

DATE: Because this building style has persisted for longer than 1,000 years, it's almost impossible to distinguish the old houses from the new.

FASCINATING FACT: Village streets were arranged in a maze-like pattern to confuse pirates and other invaders.

If you lived here, your brightly decorated home would be easy to find. With a brush or your fingertips and lots of colors, you and your mother and sisters would have painted the outside walls of your house in bold geometric patterns and shapes that look like flowers, leaves, and birds. Each house façade in your village is decorated by its family, and each has its own recognizable expression — just like a person's face.

HOUSE TYPE: Decorated houses of Ndebele. Walking down a street in this village is much like seeing a painting exhibit that tells the story of your family through pictures. The symbols in the paintings might let you know about the arrival of a neighbor's new baby, announce a marriage, or express political opinions.

MATERIALS: These round or rectangular houses are made of earth and cow dung and have thatched roofs. In the past a variety of clays, lime, soot, and earth were used to make the colors. Today, Ndebele's mural painters use brilliantly colored store-bought paints.

LOCATION: Pretoria, Transvaal, South Africa

DATE: The tradition of the decorated house dates back to the 1600s. Ndebele mothers continue to pass the custom of house painting to the next generation so that new murals are constantly being created.

FASCINATING FACT: The women of Ndebele were able to communicate secretly during times of war through the messages in their murals.

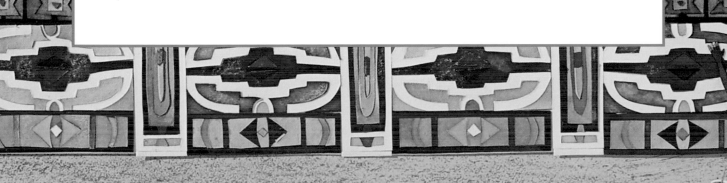

If you lived here, you could move with your family and bring your house, called a yurt, along with you. Easily taken down in an hour, a yurt is made of parts light enough for a family's horses or yaks to carry to new grazing grounds, where they are reassembled. Although the outside felt wall surrounds one large room, the yurt can be subdivided into smaller living spaces.

HOUSE TYPE: Yurt (Turkish word for "dwelling")

MATERIALS: Supporting vertical wood poles slide through a wooden ring at the top of a lattice frame, which is covered by layers of felt. The outermost layer is oiled for waterproofing and is often decorated with embroidery.

LOCATION: Throughout Mongolia and many other parts of Asia

DATE: For over 2,000 years until the present day, people have lived in yurts.

FASCINATING FACT: More than half the people of Mongolia live in yurts.

If you lived here, you could travel with your family from Alaska all the way to Florida — and always be at home. Tucked inside this trailer are foldaway beds, a small kitchen, a tiny bathroom, a sofa, chairs, and cabinets filled with food. At your doorstep, you could have a campfire at Denali National Park in Alaska or spot an alligator in the Everglades of Florida.

HOUSE TYPE: Airstream trailer

MATERIALS: Aluminum body, steel, rubber, plastic, and wood

LOCATION: Anywhere and everywhere wheels can roll. Unlike yurts, they are usually moved from place to place for vacations or pleasure rather than for livelihood.

DATE: Airstreams have been manufactured in Ohio since 1936.

FASCINATING FACT: The idea for a traveling house came from a young man named Wally Byam who lived and worked in a horse-drawn chuck wagon. Years later he traded in his wagon for a trailer when he founded the Airstream Company.

If you lived here, you could see the sunrise from your bedroom window, feel your house rotate, and later see the sunset from the same window! Using two steering wheels, you can turn your floating house to get a different view. When you want to get ashore you just scoot over on a twenty-foot-long metal gangway.

HOUSE TYPE: Floating house. Inspired by traditional Dutch houseboats, this floating design can be built in just four months.

MATERIALS: The walls, floors, and structure of the house are made of a lightweight steel with foam insulation. It sits on a frame of hollow steel tubes that is buoyant enough to support 135 tons, which help to keep the house stable in choppy waters or storms.

LOCATION: Middleburg, the Netherlands

DATE: This house was built in 1986 and is thought to be the first floating house that can rotate mechanically.

FASCINATING FACT: An early example of "green" architectural design, the house can face the sun for warmth or turn away from the sun to keep cool. Because it floats, valuable land area is not consumed.

If you lived here, in the cool of the trees, you and your friends could be high above the ground and away from your parents, brothers, and sisters. With a strong tree in your backyard, and with whatever scrap materials you can find — boards, old windows and doors, used furniture, canvas, a homemade ladder — you can build your tree house to look whatever way you like. When you finish it and climb inside with your flashlight and sleeping bag, you'll be among the squirrels and woodpeckers, and feel right at home.

FASCINATING FACT: People have built tree houses for shelter and protection since prehistoric times. Tree houses range from those in the New Guinea rain forests, built as high as 100 feet above the ground, to Italian versions from the 1600s that included marble benches and fountains. Today, whole families can live in large tree houses that have all the modern comforts of a typical home.

SELECTED SOURCES: Hubka, Thomas C. *Big House, Little House, Back House, Barn.* Hanover, N.H.: University Press of New England, 1984. • Jürgen Hansen, Hans. *Architecture in Wood.* New York: Viking Press, 1971. • Keister, Douglas. *Silver Palaces.* Salt Lake City: Gibbs Smith, 2004. • Knapp, Ronald. *Chinese Houses: The Architectural Heritage of a Nation.* North Clarendon, Vt.: Tuttle, 2005. • Nelson, Peter and Judy, and David Larkin. *The Treehouse Book.* New York: Universe Publishing, 2000. • Ököhauser, Kleine. *Small Eco-Houses.* Köln, Germany: Evergreen, 2007. • Oliver, Paul. *Dwellings: The House Around the World.* Austin: University of Texas Press, 1987. • Walker, Lester. *American Shelter.* Woodstock, N.Y.: Overlook Press, 1997. • Wheeler, Daniel, and the editors of Réalités-Hachete. *The Chateaux of France.* New York: Vendome Press, 1979.